The Executive Branch:

Leading the Way

By
Dr. Latina Campbell

Print ISBN: 978-1-966491-06-4

eBook ISBN: 978-1-966491-07-1

Printed in the United States of America

Story Corner Publishing & Consulting, Inc.

Chesapeake, VA 23321

Storycornerpublishing@yahoo.com

www.StoryCornerPublishing.com

Dedication

I dedicate this book to all the children who dream of becoming the future president, members of Congress, judges, lawyers, politicians, law enforcement, or even military. Be fair and just with everyone and do everything in love and kindness. Put God first and allow Him to lead you through every decision.

In the meantime, remember no matter who holds office or what laws are passed, God has the final say and remains in control. There's no need to worry about things you see happen in the world, just pray to God. Prayer changes everything.

P.S.

I'm proud of you because you are brave!

1

In a country so big, with states far and wide,

Who helps make sure we all stay unified?

The Executive Branch leads us each day,

Working for the people in every way.

3

This branch has a leader, strong and true,

The President of the United States—that's who!

The President's job is big and grand,

To guide our country and keep it planned.

The President signs laws to make them real,

After Congress debates and seals the deal.

But if a law doesn't seem quite right,

The President can veto it with might!

The Executive Branch has more than one face,

It's made of departments all over the place.

Each department has a special part,

From education to science and art.

The Vice President works closely, too,

Ready to help in all they do.

If the President can't lead on any day,

The Vice President steps in right away.

IN GOD WE TRUST

There's also a group, wise and bright,

Called the Cabinet, who helps shed light.

The Cabinet advises, shares what they know,

So the President can help our country grow.

The Executive Branch also keeps us secure,

With the military making our safety sure.

The President leads the armed forces strong,

Protecting our country all year long.

And don't forget about foreign lands,

The President shakes important hands.

Meeting with leaders from far and near,

To bring about peace and make things clear.

17

From signing treaties to helping trade,

The Executive Branch helps deals get made.

They work with others to show our might,

But also to spread kindness and light.

PRESIDENTIAL
ELECTION

But the President doesn't lead alone,

The people have power—our voices are known.

We vote to choose who will take the stand,

To guide our country, this amazing land.

The Executive Branch keeps things on track,

From fixing problems to having our back.

It enforces the laws and leads the way,

Making sure we're safe every day.

23

So now you know how this branch plays its part,

Leading the country with strength and heart.

The Executive Branch is important, it's true,

Helping our nation work for me and you!

The End

www.ingramcontent.com/pod-product-compliance
Lightning Source LLC
Chambersburg PA
CBHW080128150626

46550CB00017B/2832